I0518573

# PURPOSE OVER PRESSURE

# PURPOSE OVER PRESSURE

LAUREN REED

# Contents

# Purpose Over Pressure

*A student's story of ambition, anxiety, and answering her calling.*

LAUREN REED
Author

LAURENKAMORA.COM

Copyright © 2025 by Lauren Reed

All rights reserved. No part of this book may be reproduced in any manner whatsoever without written permission except in the case of brief
quotations embodied in critical articles and reviews.

First Printing, 2025

# Prelude

**B**efore We Begin

The journey between college and choosing a career is intimidating to many. For me, I was intimidated by the uncertainty of what the future held after dropping the pre-medical track to pursue a pathway leading me to a PhD. During this time, I felt lost, confused, and so many other emotions. I have come across many people in the same boat, who feel like they are completely lost, even after months of planning and meeting with advisors.

Although I was certain about pursuing a career in psychology, my initial understanding of the pathway was somewhat inaccurate. Not only is it for students interested in medical school or those interested in practicing medicine, there is also an alternative pathway to clinical psychology through specialized graduate programs dedicated to becoming a practitioner. This realization further supported the pivot of my academic plan to align with my true goals of a career as a clinical practitioner.

After having conversations with my younger sister, who is soon to graduate from high school, fellow students in classes of mine, and those I mentored in a transition seminar, I realized the stress they felt was so similar to what I was feeling, though in a different way. I was disturbed by my change of pathway to obtain a doctoral degree and work in the realm of psychology, whereas others were having difficulties deciding which field they wanted to be in altogether. That is when I realized that there was a common denominator and that students put a substantial amount of pressure on themselves to make it to the next level. For me, the pressure led me to overplanning, constantly checking my schedule, and looking for jobs for 15-20 years from now. That is what inspired me to write my latest book, *Purpose Over Pressure*.

Purpose: the goals fueling your demands and expectations

Pressure: the stress you feel from your demands and expectations

# 1

# My Plan

There I was. I bought all of the MCAT study books. I wrote down every class I needed to take for my major and to get into my dream medical school. I had every semester mapped out. I knew which classes I would take if a certain one wasn't offered that semester. I knew which classes I should add to my list, just in case I wanted to have more options and places to go after graduating. I was going to be a doctor, a psychiatrist. I loved the field of psychology and spent an extensive amount of my free time learning more about the field. I was registering for more classes than required to graduate.

Each week, I spent countless hours reviewing my plan. I needed to have it mapped out step-by-step. If not, I could miss something... right? I could accidentally not take enough classes and not get into my dream school. The best way for me to be able to help others in the field of psychology was to become a medical doctor...right? I spent hours studying for an organic chemistry class that I was learning nothing from. I pushed through. I'd already taken biology and most of the pre-med classes. I was in physics and only had to take one more physics class and a biochemistry class.

Then, I would be all set. I'd finish my psychology classes and be ready for med school.

Time was winding down, and it wouldn't be long before I needed to take the MCAT. Though I had all of the books, I was taking additional psychology classes instead of reading them. In my free time, I was teaching others fun facts about psychology and explaining the brain to my younger sister, who looked at me annoyed each time. Whenever anyone would talk about their thoughts, I'd go on a tangent about how I am a psychology student. My dad would always say, "Don't psychoanalyze me, Lauren." I was just as excited as could be. With so many years away from practicing, I used every opportunity to prepare myself for the field.

One day, I sat in my dorm, calculating what grade I needed to get in physics. I began researching if medical schools would accept a student with a C in a premed class. My first C in life was in organic chemistry, and I was on that same track in physics. I spent hours using the grade calculator, going to extra study hours, reading the physics textbook, and so on. I found more joy in planning my future than I did in anything else. I was so excited. I told myself, if I got a C in this physics class, it better be my last one. On the first test, I got a 31%. "Holy crap!" I know. After that, I started going to more study sessions, and "locking in." I told myself, if I got 50% on the next test, I could potentially get a B in the class, or at least pass it. Well, as I was waiting for my next physics lecture to start, I got a notification, "Test 2 has been graded." Guess what I got. Better by every bit of two points—a 33%. I did not go to lecture that day. I got up and walked to my dorm. I planned an advisory meeting that day. I started doing research. What job could I get in psychology without going to medical school? This was my lifelong dream. My world felt like it was crashing down.

In my advisory meeting, I sat there with tears in my eyes. I asked my advisor, what was I going to do? Was my life over? I felt like a complete failure. If I dropped this physics class, I would either have to retake it and delay my graduation date, or I would have to drop the pre-med track altogether. How was I going to become a psychiatrist now? Well, it was that day I realized my dream job was not to be a psychiatrist, and I was not going to accomplish what I was trying to accomplish by getting my MD. What I wanted was to do psychotherapy, yes. What I wanted was to help others battling the variety of mental illnesses that exist, yes. What I wanted to do was to examine the interaction between the brain and behavior, yes. What I wanted was to study psychology and neuroscience and maybe evaluate psychiatric and neurology patients in a hospital, yes. But, what I did not want to do is study the entire body. I wanted to study how the brain affects it, yes, but I really didn't care to learn how to perform surgery. I nearly pass out when I see blood or hear vomit. The job I was desperately excited to get was as a psychologist. More specifically, if I wanted to explore the cross over between psychology and neuroscience. I could specialize in neuropsychology. But how could I get the credentials and education to do this? What I needed was a PhD. So yes, I'd still be Dr. Reed, just not with an MD.

Okay. So now, I need to plan every single thing all over again. I need to map out exactly how I am going to get there, figure out where I am going to go to graduate school, and what I need to do now to make sure that I am certain to get accepted. With this outcasted C on my transcript, how could I fix this? During this seemingly life-altering decision, I came to the conclusion that physics was not "hard." Granted I was taking the class at the hardest school in the state, but it wasn't *that* it was hard. It was that I just didn't want to do it. Yes, I know we all have to take classes we aren't interested in. But, it didn't align with my goals. I would spend hours rewriting my cognitive neuroscience notes, making extra Power-Point to review, quizzing myself, asking others to quiz me, making flashcards, going to office hours, asking questions that went beyond the scope of the class, and doing everything possible to *learn*, not just get an A. While my grades were important, I wanted to carry this knowledge with me to grad school.

Now that is how my life changed, and I realized that I didn't get that C for nothing. It was a life lesson. When I withdrew from that physics class at the last minute, it was time for me to reevaluate how I could achieve my lifelong goal of helping others. Of course, I met with my advisor nearly every two weeks, constantly dropped into his office hours, and made advisory meetings with anyone who was offering them. I was scared. I'd never made such a decision in my life. I didn't even want to tell my mom that she spent $200 on MCAT books for nothing and my dad that I was lost in life. But, when I told my parents they said to me something I'd never thought I'd hear. They explained to me that I'd put in so much effort and that they were just proud I was getting my bachelor's degree. My mom said who cares if you get a C and that I'd be fine by staying in the class and my dad said if it's stressing you then drop it. Obviously, they are polar opposites, but they both agreed that I'd put in so much work to get to this point that I had the luxury of taking time to think.

Now that I got the not so scary conversation with my parents out of the way, it was time for me to start planning this PhD track that I'd chosen. After doing some research, I actually realized that I would have been miserable getting my MD and that the PhD was what I wanted all along. I'd be able to practice, research, and teach if I wanted to. This was game-changing. Okay, now I needed to research all of the PhD schools in my comfort zone. This was only after learning that I must get a PhD in clinical psychology and that I couldn't stay at Tech. This was another devastating moment for me. Anyways, I pushed through that and learned that my dream med school also offered a clinical PhD. I also learned that it was likely that I would still be involved with med school, as my neuropsych fellowship would be done here. Okay, that's not such bad news. Well, now that I dropped the pre-med track, what's next? I guess now is a good time to mention that I declared two minors to sub for the pre-med classes that were no longer in my plan. For the record, this was so uncalled for, and I did not need to do this. But, me being the overly ambitious girlie that I am, I decided to do it anyway. Not to brag. I actually learned a lot about myself. It wasn't that I couldn't handle the rigor. I replaced each pre-med class with two other classes. Meaning, that I was actually going to take on a heavier load. Okay, but now since I figured out where I'm going to go, I can stop planning now right?

# 2

# Angst

What I had to realize was that each time I went on these over-planning tangents, my heart rate was elevated, my mind was running a thousand miles per minute, and I would stop doing schoolwork just to tend to these thoughts. I was sending my stress levels through the roof, which is extremely unhealthy both physically and mentally. But this was helping me prepare for my future right? When you are in high school everyone tells you that you should know what you want to be and do in life. "Now's the time," they say. So, I thought this was just the same. The thing is, I already figured it out. I made a change and everything was fine. I was already taking the classes that I needed, I'd already picked out my grad schools, and I was on track to graduate. Well, that wasn't enough, then I wanted to know which internships I needed to complete, how long I'd spend in grad school, which fellowship I would do, and where I would work after that. Obviously, I was being prepared and smart... right?

Of course it is important to plan things out. However, it got to a point where I was constantly overthinking about where I was going to go and what I needed to do. I always felt like I needed to be doing more and that I wasn't doing enough. I had a fear of messing up my future. I didn't want to waste any time or fail to do something pertinent to my career. It took some getting used to, not knowing which school I was going to get into and there being so many unknowns. I'd constantly write it down and keep rewriting it. There was always room for improvement in this plan.

I hadn't even acknowledged the relief I felt from all of the premed stress and my disdain for chemistry. I'd already given myself something else to worry about. It was a never-ending cycle of anxiety, planning, researching all of my options, then, planning, anxiety, planning, researching all of my options, planning, anxiety... you get it. This was so emotionally taxing. By the time I was done, I'd wanted to enroll myself in five new classes, take on a double major, and I even considered getting an associate's in Spanish during the process. While I do believe that I could have done all of those things and succeeded, I also believe that my stress would have become even worse. If you know anything about psychology, you know that stress has so many negative effects on the mind, the body, and makes it pretty darn hard to get work done.

Though this seemed like I was planning things out and being orderly to some, on the inside, I felt like I was drowning in my thoughts. I was overwhelming myself with the countless possibilities. I had to realize it is okay to choose just one thing. I had to realize that it is okay to not have my life planned out for the next ten years and that I needed to focus on getting into grad school and worry about the rest once I got there. So, planning was important, yes, but just not to the degree that I was doing it. I was looking at every grad school I wanted to apply to, what internships they offer, how they train you to do psychotherapy, which fellowships they offer and how they train their fellows, if they have job openings in my field of interest, how I could work my way up to becoming a professor, what research I needed to do for my dissertation, and the application process. All I needed to do was identify the grad school and determine whether or not they have the specialties that I am interested in, then worry about the application process, and save the rest for later. If I was going to jot down some notes about all of things, I did not need to do it all at once. I needed to give myself time to focus on my studies and spend a *little* bit of time doing research on grad schools, given I had months before the applications opened and the schools hadn't released potential faculty for me to choose from as my PhD advisor.

Some people may be able to plan things out in this vicious manner, but for me, it was causing me more stress than my organic chemistry and physics classes combined. I needed to relax. It seemed so easy to get engulfed in all of the thoughts that were flowing through my mind. So, what did I do? You may be thinking, "keep overplanning." However, I actually found a way to deal with these worries and plan at the same time. Whenever I would have a thought that I was not planning things out properly or enough, I would write down my plan in very few words and determine what my next step was. For example, if my plan was B.S., PhD, internship, dissertation, graduation, fellowship, practice in the field... Then, I would write that out and determine what I needed to work on. Obviously, I do not know which schools will accept me or which one I will ultimately say yes to. So, right now, I need to check the application requirements for them and go from there. There would be no need to figure out exactly which internship and so on I would do, as I know that each one that I am applying to at least fits one of my interests.

Surprisingly, recognizing these self-sabotaging thoughts and writing them down helped clear my mind and allowed me to focus on my studies so much better. If you are in the same boat, be it in a career change, moving homes, or deciding what to eat for dinner, recognize these thoughts. The worst thing to ever do is to sit there and allow them to overpower your thought process and functioning. Write them down. You'd be surprised with how many of your thoughts are actually the same thought, just written in a different font. Then, half of your "problems" will be eliminated, merely because they never really existed. Then, you can prioritize them and decide which battle you want to fight first.

One thing I must note is that some people see this as completely normal to overplan and others see no need to plan at all. For me, it was not that I *needed* to plan or that I planned too much. It was that I was not effectively dealing with the emotions and thoughts that came with this planning. I am a person who likes to have plans and prefers to know how things are going to go. This was exacerbated by the change of pathways to my graduate journey. A lot of the time, we do not properly handle a situation simply because we are not correcting the right problem. Planning was not the problem, the thoughts around it were. I had to realize that these were anxious thoughts of me not wanting to let myself down. This was all a battle within. I felt like I was starting from the bottom. I spent years thinking about what my specialty would be as I progressed in med school. Then, to just completely cancel those plans was a huge change for me.

At last, my thoughts were coming from my desire to succeed and reach my full potential. I wanted to learn everything possible about psychology and thought that I was doing so by going to medical school. Little did I realize that much of the emphasis on psychology would not be for years later when I picked a specialty. Not only that, I would have had to dissect God knows what and spend hours learning about the cardiovascular system, which was far from my interests in psychology. Then, I realized that my desire to take way more psychology classes than required for a B.S. was driven by my ultimate goal to get an advanced education in the field. What better way to do this than to get a PhD? Though this was the case, the angst remained and I had to shake it by tending to my thoughts mindfully and truthfully by recognizing my fear of change and ambiguity.

# 3

# Direction

Though my plans changed, it took me a while to realize it really didn't. My end game remained the same, and the only thing that changed was how I was going to reach my goal. During my college career, I have helped many people find their way in deciding their major, which classes they should take, etc. In many of my conversations, people explain to me that they just don't know what they want to do and that they want to be like me and have everything all figured out. They ask me how I do it. Little do they know, most of the time I am stressed *because* I know what I want to do. I tell them just like I will tell you, you do not have to know exactly what you want to do or where you want to be. Being a psychology major, I often cross paths with declared neuroscience and biomedical engineering (BME) majors. They often express not knowing what job they want to do after graduating and explain to me just how scary and frustrating it is to have no idea where they will be in just a few years from now.

Whether you are trying to figure out "this or that," for where to move, which job to take, what to have for dinner every day next week, what to major in in college, where to go to graduate school, or simply which class to take over the other, take things one step at a time. What I like to say is, figure out what all of your options have in common, and work on that first. For example, all of my grad school applications have certain requirements, one of them being to graduate with your bachelor's degree first. So, instead of writing my statement of purpose right now, I need to figure out which classes I am going to take in the upcoming semesters to accomplish my first task, graduating. For you, you may be considering applying to one of three jobs that each have a long list of qualifications and certifications. Instead of trying to do all of the certifications for each job, work on the certification that they all have in common while you figure out the pros and cons of each job. That way, you are still heading in the direction of your goal. It really can be that simple.

We do not have to have everything mapped out, and honestly, it's probably better not to. For me, when I decided to take the psychology path, I was not certain what I wanted to specialize in. I truly believe if I'd chosen health psychology and never looked anywhere else, or explored my interests first, I would have never considered neuropsychology. I took some psychology classes, when I say "some" I mean all that I possibly could, then I realized I had a keen interest in the overlap between the brain and behavior. From here, I did some research and figured out that this lies in the scope of what a neuropsychologist does. Granted, I still have not put this set in stone in my mind and have plenty of time to choose a different specialty. My point is I am going in that direction either way, so it really doesn't matter which one I choose at this moment.

For you, identify a long-term goal of yours, the steps it takes to get there, and highlight the first step you should take. Of course, there is nothing wrong with jotting down some notes about the other steps. But there is really no use in worrying about how you will decorate the desk you will sit at in a job you haven't gotten, let alone a degree that has yet to be obtained to meet the job qualifications, or the classes for the degree. You get where I'm going.

Or you can simply write down what is left to get to the first step, which may be obtaining a certification, taking your core classes to get any degree of any major, or finishing the classes you are currently taking. Essentially, to reach any long-term goal, we must just go in that direction. The rest will come as we progress and take the necessary steps. We must allow ourselves to have this flexibility, or else we may limit ourselves and ultimately, the careers we have to choose from.

# 4

# My Choice

In a battle of anxious thoughts about how I can craft the perfect plan, I often looked for answers elsewhere. I'd spend hours on Google trying to craft this perfect plan. Let me just say, I got so many mixed messages from the Internet, yet I continued searching for this perfect plan. This was the closest I could get to getting some answers. My advisors always ended their advice with "but I cannot make a decision for you." Since the Internet varies across sites, just one word can make a message the wrong advice, yet it was sufficient enough to help with some of these anxious thoughts... until it wasn't.

I'd even tried asking my dad, the person who thinks most like me. The smartest man I know, yet he still told me he couldn't tell me what grad school to pick and help me craft this perfect career plan. My mom is so good with technology, sometimes I question which one of us grew up without it. Yet, she couldn't find these answers online with me either. Though she did go through PhD advisors in various clinical programs when I asked her to look at them with me. Yet, none of us could come up with a definite answer as to where Lauren should go and how she should go about fulfilling these lifelong goals of hers.

Eventually, I started planning again. This time, using the techniques I'd taught myself to avoid being overwhelmed in the process. I'd write things down right away, rather than sitting in angst for hours. Then, I said, "wait a minute." I was spending all of this time trying to plan things out and stressing as if I was going to fall off of a bridge if I didn't have a fifteen-year plan and each step detailed out on a piece of paper. I could take my time. I hadn't even given myself a congratulations that I was accepted into the master's program at Tech. So, even if I decided to get my master's then apply to the PhD programs, I would be fine. I could use this as time to gather my thoughts and act as an intermittent step to prepare for my PhD application cycle. After all, I was getting my bachelor's degree in three years and was racing a clock that literally did not exist.

During this race, I felt completely lost and submerged under the stress I was causing myself. It took me so long to realize that I was at my dream school, conducting research, learning more about the field that I love, had some extra time to write, and did not have to make a decision about graduate school for at least another year. That is of course if I went with the master's. As I write this, I am still unsure whether I will go straight into my PhD, or obtain my master's degree in cognition and brain science first, before going into the clinical field. Having this uncertainty doesn't make me any less of a person, nor does it make me a failure. These are both great options that hold significant pros. There is certainly no con to getting another year of education, except for the fact that it may be tens of thousands of dollars, but other than that... That being said, why was I so stressed then? Something I have learned in my few years of studying psychology is that stress depends on how you perceive a situation. Think of a phobia, someone may be extremely terrified of spiders and have a severe stress response and maybe a panic attack if they see one. Someone else may just kill the spider. Well, uncertainty is my spider and sends me into a panicked state when I feel like things are not mapped out. Of course, this is out of my control, but I had to learn how to effectively deal with these stressors. In my journey of dedicating my life to psychology, I have also decided to take a few tips as well. It only makes sense for me to learn how to effectively manage my stress and anxious thoughts if I want to help others do the same.

How ironic is it that not knowing what I want to do caused me just as much stress as knowing what I want to do? Very ironic. This goes to show that the problem lies not in knowing where you will be in ten years, but in the way that you think about the next ten years. I have spent so much time geared toward figuring things out, that it would ultimately be a waste if I changed my mind even a little. That is the power in doing things one step at a time, because as you change within each stage, you will be slightly changing the steps that follow.

I'm not doing this for anyone other than myself. I have already made my parents proud by going to Tech, getting a bachelor's degree and never having a gpa that doesn't represent highest honors. Of course, if you haven't done those things that does not mean you are any less of an individual or any less amazing. These are just the things that *my* parents asked of me. To add to this, I am sure they are not nearly as thrilled as I am about getting at least two more degrees in psychology, especially considering they are tired of hearing about the brain. My mom was reading a research proposal that I wrote and said, "What the hell is an anterior cingulate cortex?" I had to remember that she is not a neuroscience student and that not everyone gives a crap about mastering the double dissociation between Wernicke's and Broca's area. Don't worry if you have no idea what that is.

It was almost like being freed of those pre-med stressors gave me a completely different outlook on life. I started to understand the importance of choosing something you love rather than following the trend. Growing up, I always knew I wanted to help. It started with my drive to be a veterinarian, then an anesthesiologist. This was before I was in middle school, so of course I didn't know what psychology was. Then, life happened and I took AP psychology in high school and knew that *this* is what I wanted to do. This was my calling. However, all I knew was: med school + psychology = psychiatrist. Though this is "true," there are other possibilities. I should have said: grad school + psychology = career in the field of psychology. That would have given me all of my bachelor years to figure this out. Of course, I would have needed to talk to some advisors about my plan at some point, but this would have helped me see many more options and kept me from feeling like a complete failure and as if my life was over when I dropped physics.

This freedom inspired me to use my helping skills now, as I did not want to wait to help others until I was 30. Obviously, I am not nearly qualified to diagnose anyone with a mental illness, teach anyone psychology, and I still have to check "high school diploma" on Indeed. However, I can do so much now as well. So far, I have taken on three (and plan to do a fourth) volunteer, team-leader positions in Georgia Tech's transition seminar program to help incoming freshman and transfer students have a seamless welcome to the GT climate, because let me tell you, it can be cold.

When I went to orientation, I didn't think it was important to take the class and didn't think twice about taking it. "I got this," I thought, and I was able to successfully plan and register for all of my classes after meeting with my academic advisor. I also maintained amazing grades and a heavy course load, maxing out my credits almost every semester. I knew what I wanted to be when I graduated, and though my path changed a bit, I also had a pretty good plan to get there. However, after watching my younger sister go through the junior to senior high school transition and preparation for college applications, I realized it is not as seamless for everyone as it was for me. This is what inspired me to apply for the position as soon as it hit my inbox. London, if you ever read this, I want you to know I am very proud of you and cannot wait to see all of the great things you will do in life.

Given we had all of the help and support in the world, I can only imagine the struggle of those who lack it. I hope to touch as many hearts as I can and help them feel that warm and cozy support during an emotionally taxing transition in life. As excited as I am, I still have times when I am filled with angst when I think of the possibility of having to go to a new school, let alone potentially having to go out of state for a grad program. I can only imagine the stress and thoughts of someone who is going through such a transition, not having any clue as to what they want to major in, and especially having no clue as to what career they'd like. I told my sister, who was in the same position, to think about some things that she finds interesting in school and outside of school. There she was, all by herself picking out a potential major in college. She was actually excited to have experienced this. She went back and told my parents she knew what she wanted to major in *and* what she wanted to be. Sometimes it is not that we do not know what we want to be, but we are unsure of how to describe it or reach that conclusion without a bit of guidance. No matter what stage we get to in our lives, we will never have all of the answers. It is up to us how we will seek them and at what point we will be content with the answers that we do have.

# 5

# Reaching Out

My parents are both first-generation college students, and my mom is a first-generation graduate student. However, neither of my parents work in the medical field and did not study anything related to psychology. Yet and still, I had all the support I needed during my undergraduate studies. However, I will be a first-generation doctoral student and the only person in my family to study psychology. So, I could only get so far with the help of my parents, though I don't think I'd be in the position that I am in now without them. Anyway, I said that to say that even if you have a great support system and educated parents, you will still likely need to reach out for assistance.

For me, I did not have a single friend going into college. Of course, I am still cordial with people from high school, but I haven't seen or hung out with anyone from high school after my first year of college. To make things worse, I didn't know anyone that went to Tech, at least not enough to hang out with them. I was also a bit shy and did not join any clubs nor did I do the transition seminar during my first year at Tech. So, it was up to me to get the support that I needed. Easier said than done of course, but we must craft our academic support team. I reached out to several professors and practitioners who were in my field of interest. I met with my advisor so many times, I started to wonder if I was meeting with him too often. It's not easy to ask for help, especially when you don't even know which questions to ask. There were plenty of days where I'd go into a professor's office and just tell them my academic and career plans to see if it even logically went together. During my MD journey, I considered getting an MD/PhD. When I dropped the pre-med track, I was planning to get my PhD at Tech, or at least applying. Then, I realized that the PhD must be in clinical psychology and not in cognition and brain science and that it does in fact matter the concentration that you choose.

This was a huge deal, as I would not have been eligible for a license to do my dream job. I didn't know this and neither did anyone in my family. We all crafted this plan, yet we still needed to reach out for clarification and assistance with this plan. Now, I meet with my advisor every time he has drop-in hours. One time, I dropped by his office three times in one day. To be fair, I had some good questions. The point is, don't be afraid to reach out for help, even if it's not from an academic advisor. I meet with professors, people in the mental health resource center, advisors, and more. There is nothing wrong with having a holistic plan, especially when it comes to your future. Each conversation that I have, I realize that I could have been on a completely different journey without it. You only know so much, and it is important to recognize that. Also, if you are paying tens of thousands of dollars to go to a university, even if it is scholarship money, you might as well use the resources that you are paying for.

Even if you don't have any questions, it is still good to check in and make sure that you are on the right track or that you are not missing any opportunities to explore and grow. That was my main thing. I was always on track to graduate and so on, but I needed to network and reach out to gain more information about the endless resources and opportunities on campus. One semester at Tech, I took a class called neuroscience of mental health, taught by a licensed clinical psychologist and the chair of psychology. Not only was the class insightful, but taking it led me to make some of the most cherished connections that I may ever have in my career. "How?" you may ask. Well, the licensed clinical psychologist allowed me to come into her office, spill all of my thoughts about grad school, and have a better idea of what it's like to be a clinical psychologist. On another occasion, I was scrolling through the registration portal and saw a class, computational neuroscience. I reached out to the professor, who was also the chair that was co-teaching the class I referred to, to inquire about the class. This reaching out led me to join a lab of people who make me feel welcomed, collaborate with an amazing research advisor who is always happy to answer my abundance of questions, and potentially will advise and endorse my master's research thesis. Might I add my mentor is a very well trusted and respected global leader in academia, whom I will be forever grateful for.

Now, everytime I have these rush of thoughts and questions, I ask them. I write them down first, of course. But, I use these questions to my advantage. Rather than allowing myself to undergo a substantial amount of stress and worry, I look at my very well-crafted plan and see how these questions can enhance it. However, I have also developed the patience to allow these questions to eventually be answered by a knowledgeable person, rather than some random website online. If you are like me and have this weight of ambiguity, allow yourself to find calmness in this storm and to use these thoughts in a creative way. For example, I have so many questions about grad school. I am also extremely excited and nervous about it. I have researched many of them myself and asked my academic advisor a few of my questions as well, but my most important questions are still written down. Instead of allowing this to eat me alive, I reached out to my research advisor, who I now have a meeting with this upcoming Wednesday. Writing these questions down not only allowed me to fit them into my career plan, but encouraged me to organize them so that when I do ask them, they do not overwhelm the person on the receiving end. That goes back to my point of the importance of acknowledging your thoughts, writing them down, and tending to them a little at a time. This has removed an enormous amount of stress off of me, and I am certain that it will do the same for you if you find yourself in these shoes.

# 6

## Letting Things Fall In Line

During my last semester as a junior, I applied for a position to get clinical experience. The job would train me to be a medical scribe and take notes on doctor-patient interactions. "This was perfect," I thought. I'd finally get to see the day in the life of a doctor. I hoped everyday that the doctor would be a psychiatrist, or maybe a neurologist. This was my step closer to my dream job... so I thought. I ended up not taking the job due to a conflict. In hindsight, it seems like the job just wasn't for me. After months of worrying, spending hours a day trying to figure out what was right for me, I finally saw that I was already doing what I loved. I was already in the positions that I wanted to be in. I was on the right track and did not need to continuously overload myself.

In reality, I was overcompensating for what I thought was a lack of experience and attractability for graduate schools. Yet, I was stretching myself thin with the overwhelming tasks I'd given myself. It took a while for me to realize that I was doing enough and that I needed to be patient. I needed to allow myself time to accomplish these tasks before I picked up a few more. I could not stand the abundance of free time and felt guilty for doing as much as taking a break to eat dinner. So, what'd I do? I took more classes the following semester. Eventually, I ran out of classes to sneak into my schedule.

This was really another indicator that a PhD was far more suited for me than going to medical school. Though I said that I was in fact overloading myself at times, I must also acknowledge that it was for a darn good reason. It wasn't that I couldn't handle my ambition or my work load. Rather, it was that my ambition was strictly in psychology. It took so long for me to realize that my interest was not a subset of medical school. My specialty is a subset of my interest. What I mean is that psychology is my passion, yes. I want to get a doctorate, yes. But, I want to get a doctorate in psychology, with a specialization in the brain and behavior. I do not want to study the entire human existence, with a specialty in psychology. That would not be in-depth enough for my interests. I have a strong love for the subject. I want to practice it, teach it, and so much more.

This is good though, right? Knowing what I wanted to do and finally understanding that this is the path that I wanted to take should have brought me peace and tranquility. Well, let me just say it was far from that. It brought me so many new ideas that I'd never heard of before. I didn't know many of these fields existed. I put a barrier on myself and pushed myself so far in a direction to try and be the perfect "doctor" that I didn't realize that my passions did not lie there. Then, to be faced with such a huge change in direction, let alone trying to figure out how to come back from this devastating C in organic chemistry.

I couldn't shake all of these rushes of thoughts around graduating, and where I was going to go. They'd often circle back and send me down a spiral of panic. Every time registration information would be sent out for classes, I'd spend hours planning again. Though this time it was different... right? I must plan out my classes and ensure I stay on track to graduate, especially since certain classes are only offered during certain semesters. Well, yes, but also not when it takes hours out of my day to arrange a "maybe" schedule for next semester. I had to become aware of these self-sabotaging thoughts that ran through my mind all day, causing me to become so focused on the future that I had to spend all night catching up on my work for my current classes. It was so challenging though. What if I had another change of plans?

All of the "what ifs" and "maybes" needed to go. They were becoming so irrelevant in my life. I'd already crafted a plan and ran it by advisors. What more could I do? Well, if you asked me at that time, I'd have given you a list of things. But looking at things now, absolutely nothing. I worked ahead for so long that when I finally reached an end point, it was so scary to just do nothing. I took on extra classes and extracurricular activities, I started to make friends, and things finally started to slow down. Of course, I still work weeks in advance and stay far ahead of my work, so I often have "extra" time on my hands. But if you're a Yellow Jacket, then you know that I spend every ounce of free time raving about my new learnings from my classes or rewriting my notes to prepare for an exam. My point is, that after all of the exhausting worrying settled down, I was finally about to appreciate the joys in life. Given that I only had a short time in college, it would be advisable for me to enjoy these years, try and make some friends, and at least make my way out of my dorm.

Well, since I worked so hard to get a few minutes of free time, I might as well use them doing something other than worrying about a future I have already figured out. As I started taking time to explore campus, get out of my dorm, and get my head out of my books, I started joining clubs, doing some real networking, and learning about ways to actually advance my career, which proved far more beneficial than writing out a plan for the twenty thousandth time. Things began to come together so smoothly. Just a few months prior, I was applying for three to four positions at a time, half of the time being ghosted by employers for not having enough experience. Now, I am able to take this with a grain of salt and move on to the next best thing. Moral of the story is, I just needed to give things a chance to work out for me and have confidence in myself.

# 7

## Brighter Days

Suddenly, the skies were brighter, the days felt breezy, and you might have seen me with a smile on some days. I began using the meditation techniques I'd learned in one of the extra classes I took. I started reading books about mental health and well-being. I even started using some of the well-being activities outside of the classroom. I started nurturing my own mental health. After all, it would be ideal for me to keep my mental health in check while trying to help others do the same. All of the long nights, exhausting study sessions, and feelings of isolation seemed to be worth it. Is this what a major life change feels like? It is true that some people may be able to successfully move away to college and this change seem minute. However, when you add another major change onto that, all hell could break loose, as it did for me.

When I finally stopped overworking myself, I felt a weight lifted off my chest. To this day, I still work ahead and go above and beyond to study. However, this leaves me with days where I can do nothing if I really wanted to. Sometimes, I just have days where I have to do less. For me, it was choosing these days and not allowing myself to take this time off that was the problem. I found myself working overtime on holiday breaks, as this was my opportunity to get even more ahead. This is a good idea.. right? Well yes, it's a great idea, if you're not already several chapters ahead and just overloading yourself with work out of a fear of not doing enough. I am an overly diligent worker and give everything my all. However, sometimes after giving it my all, I try to give more. It makes it difficult for me to acknowledge my accomplishments. I remember reading my master's acceptance letter and having no emotion, as I was so stressed about changing my career path. In reality, this was extra time for me to figure things out, while advancing my education. However, I was so caught up in my self-criticism that I did not cherish this moment.

Obviously, if I am writing about it, I took some self-recognition and have a different perspective now. All of these long days weren't for nothing. I finally understood myself. I finally realized that I had so much potential and just didn't want to be a chemist. I also realized that I was not one of those people who hates working or hates school. I actually love it. I already knew this, but now it was time for me to embrace it. I also learned that I am not good friends with this thing in life called "change."

I'm one of those people who likes to make plans before going out, rather than just going on random spontaneous adventures. As you can imagine, this was my vision for my college journey, leading into my future career. However, having such a limited view on the world, it was important for me to be open to new ideas. I'm actually extremely happy that I picked my major way back when, and made it clear what my interests were. Yet, it still would have been nice to explore jobs in psychology and understand all of my options. I didn't know anything about a PhD. As far as I knew, a PhD was best for subjects that were *not* on the MCAT.

One of the most important lessons that I learned in my journey was that I needed to be adaptable and understand that change was inevitable, especially considering I was approaching the end of my undergraduate journey. Being open to change has led me to take on new opportunities, such as being a team leader of groups of students in a transition program. Before I graduated high school, I feared the class for public speaking so much that I considered not going to college at all. Of course, this was only in the moment, as I was a sophomore with dreams of becoming a doctor. Now, I am on track to lead several sections of a class full of students, defend a thesis in order for me to graduate, and hopefully teach a class of my own one day.

Though there are still many years between now and the days where I will be licensed to practice, embracing my journey and enjoying each step of the way has allowed me to feel free. Sure, I think about my future often, and sometimes I even worry about it. But at this point, I have found a common middle ground where I can do so without spending hours stressing about it. As I enjoy the journey, I have paid closer attention to detail. I have become more interested in the smaller opportunities, some that may turn out to be not so small after all.

Of course, it is often that I return to my pattern of worrying and wanting to have a concrete plan. Those are the best days for me to reflect and externalize these thoughts and use them to make a difference in life, at least I believe I am. In my time of reflection, I choose to spend my time searching for opportunities that I *can* accomplish, not saying that I cannot accomplish the others. Rather, just not right now. I visited a new lab and loved it. Will this be the lab that I end up defending my dissertation in? I'd like to think so. But what good does worrying about that serve me? None at all. Instead, I ensure that I am the best that I can be at those lab visitations, from asking questions to doing background research. This will help me determine my next steps and learn what I'm looking for in a program.

I have found that time moves so much quicker now and things seem to fall right into place. Afterall, going directly into a program is not my all-or-nothing. I didn't realize the endless directions my life could take, from changing from pre-med to pre-grad, from looking at PhD advisors to making lab visits, from finding clinical experience to getting involved with research. By looking back, I was writing my story correctly, just giving it the wrong title and headline.

# 8

# God's Plan

Was it God's plan all along that I didn't take those positions? All of the nights I spent flattened by my disdain for physics. To be honest, it was nothing like my high school physics class, which I kept all the notes for to ensure I did well in college. Let's just say... that didn't work out very well. During the same month I would've started my position as a medical scribe, I connected with my research advisor. During the very month that I felt lost and hopeless, confused and ambiguous, I got my master's acceptance letter. During my desperate search for a research advisor in grad school, I found a lab that was directly aligned with my career goals. During the time I wasn't able to get the teaching assistantship, I became a transition leader for incoming students. During the time that I felt like I had nothing to do, I had a much needed brain break. After spending countless hours getting ahead, I crashed and needed a four-day break with no screen time.

Every challenge, and seemingly barrier, was an opportunity for me to be grateful. I realized there was a problem when I found myself not even the slightest bit joyous from my greatest accomplishments. By taking on a new perspective, I have learned myself. Of course, if I plan on helping others learn themselves, I must be willing to dig deep and do the work as well. With my new attitude, I felt on top of the world, unstoppable. I even found myself going out of my way for others. I'd like to think of myself as a kind and considerate person before that, but now I was being an even better me. I'd get excited to see a message pop up on my screen from a fellow student asking me for help with something. Was this my purpose? Was I being slowed down so that I'd be able to be in this position to help others?

Technology and I aren't the best of friends, at least not yet. It took a good minute for me to take advantage of the various apps offered for hand-written notetaking. Yet, there I was taking a computer science class. Just to be clear, this was not willingly, but I do want to graduate. One day, I knew nothing, and when I say nothing I mean that I might as well not even bother opening the computer. The next, I was able to write a code so good I literally looked up to my room's ceiling and said, "Thank you!" with my hands together. I felt God walking me through those problems. While I am a strong believer in psychology, this was different. This was not the general, "sleep will consolidate your memories." This was heavenly. The code was so beautiful and flawless I had to reread it several times to ensure I wrote it.

# 9

# My Calling

The magnetism between me and the submit button on the registrar's website for any course beginning with "PSYC" is extremely strong, yet that is not nearly close to what I refer to as my drive for psychology. In a conversation I had with a career advisor, I explained my long-term career goal of becoming a clinical neuropsychologist. We came to the conclusion that my goal is to help others live a more productive life. I couldn't have thought of a better way to put it. Now I will say, I am nearly running out of psych courses to take, but for me it's far more than that. There are so many interconnections and overlaps between various mental illnesses. Even in conversations I've had with psychology majors and professors, I'd sometimes hit a roadblock when I'd used certain terms. That is how I realized that my interest was deeper than thoughts and feelings. I am enthused by the way that an anxious thought can lead to a fast heart beat, which can lead to rumination, which can lead to mental fatigue, which can lead to a spike in cortisol levels, which can lead to extreme loss of appetite, then sudden hunger. From here, you can lose motivation from the fact that a simple thought sent you down this deep rabbit hole, now you've lost your motivation, have brain fog... you get the point.

Another way to put it is neuropsychopathology. Of course, that is a long word that many people don't just have in their back pocket. Yet, the thrill of thinking of this word drives my desire to learn more. I am not an expert in the matter and nearly speculate from briefly touching the topics during the few years that I've been in college. After all of those long, exhausting exams, I am only eager for the ones in... you guessed it psychology and neuroscience, or a mixture of the two.

I have noticed that things can be one of two ways, either extremely planned out or not planned out at all. Of course, there are plenty of people in the middle. Not to toot my own horn, but it is often that people congratulate me and feel overwhelmed that I have the next twenty years of my life planned out. The truth is, behind all of these plans is so much angst and overplanning. Sometimes I wish I could just take it two steps at a time, rather than three or four. Right now, I know which graduate schools I want to go to, potential advisors, what specialty I want to do my post-doc fellowship in, a potential post-doc degree after that, along with two or three jobs that I may try to do all at once. Of course, that is overly ambitious, more than ten years from now, and will take time to work my way up to that. How could I possibly be overwhelmed about next year when I have the next ten written down? I still ask myself the same question.

Though I am still ambiguous about what the future holds and often revisit my plans, I have come to a bit of a middle ground, though it leans closer to overplanning than it does relaxation. That is just me. Finally, I could take a breath by realizing that I can take a day or two without thinking about the career I will hold and the impact I will make in twenty years. Don't ask me where all of this pressure came from, because that would point the finger directly at me. Some people find themselves overly pressured by family expectations and whatnot. For me, I've already exceeded those expectations and am putting the pressure on myself.

This brings me back to my point. Ultimately, I just needed clarity. Of course, I could change my mind anyday. However, the general basis of my goals has remained the same for the past three years, making it clear that I am heading toward my end goal, even if it changes just a little. So, I have no idea what the future holds... I said I want to be a psychologist, not a psychic. Either way, I have to give myself credit.

# 10

# Move On

Enough about Lauren and psychology. It goes beyond that. In just two months I have connected with so many fellow students, many of which have not decided their goal for the next two years. Yet, there I was stressing about my life after obtaining my PhD. I was moving so fast, I forgot about the "little things," which actually ended up being not so little. I'd wanted to hurry up and have this perfect resume. I'd sent it to many people, never once asking for a true professional opinion. Of course, I'd ask a few people here and there. Then, I took an assessment based on my resume and found that it is far from tailored to where I am in life, let alone where I want to be. When I saw these results, I felt embarrassed and almost ashamed. How could I have not taken the time to perfect my LinkedIn profile and my resume? How could I have not taken the time to notice that I was being so vague, yet hoping for so much? I guess it was more embarrassing, considering that I had so many resources sitting right in front of me. I should have been spending my time on current self-development and growth, rather than thinking about what I wanted to do in years that go past the next decade. That was a hard lesson for me. I'd been neglecting so many opportunities, because I felt that they were too minute and would not hold enough weight in the long run. Well, it turns out that I was wrong and needed to view my life from a different perspective.

Replaying scenarios in my head would not get me to my destination. Rather, I'd have to reach out, make connections, and see where life goes. That is how I began asking the right questions to the right people. Still, of course, I never got a definite answer about which application cycle I should begin applying to PhD programs. At least this time around, I was much closer to making any progress. No one can see my notes and thoughts. I needed to take risks. That is so much more productive than wasting time on Google and overthinking. Sure, assessing my long-term goals are essential to ensure that I am staying on track. It's the hours spent doing that instead of studying, then stressing about having so much work to do. I am not one to procrastinate, so I often find myself with extra time to do things like overthink and stress myself out. Still, that does me no good and sends my heart rate to the triple digits.

By focusing on factors in my "right now" and seemingly simple opportunities, I opened the door to make an impact that I didn't know I could make. I also took the time to ask people questions about their own experiences. That gives far more insight than a simple Google search, that may or may not give you an AI-generated response. I needed to hear the background. I needed to *learn* what it truly means to be a clinical psychologist. I needed to sit in a lab that talks about the depressed patients and neurotransmitter changes. That was me making progress and advancing in my "career." As an undergraduate student with no degree, how could I be stressed about finding a job that required a doctorate? Exactly. I should have been focusing on how to get as much undergraduate experience so that when the time comes, I can showcase all of my overachieving activities and the work that I am constantly putting in to achieve these goals and get these positions.

I called this chapter "Move On" not because I moved on from my goals and preparation to achieve them. Instead, I needed to move on to the things that I could change and advance, such as specializing or adding to my degree, gaining volunteer experience, and working on my own well-being. I'm sure by now you can understand why having everything "figured out" did not do much for me and my stress levels. I do not believe that I will ever be someone who is comfortable with not having things planned out with steps, however I was able to overcome my desire to keep planning and planning and planning and planning. And to those who had to answer the same questions over the course of multiple meetings, thank you.

I hope that if you find yourself in this same boat, you can realize that all you can do is be the best version of yourself at this stage, and prepare for the stages to come. Don't exhaust yourself by stressing over things that may or may not fall in line later. I finally understood this when I spent hours studying for my organic chemistry exam and got a grade below 40. I am so good with numbers, yet don't remember the grade on any of my exams in that class. Was I mad at myself? Nope, not at all. I had to realize that I did my best. Now, had I not tried my hardest and studied until I couldn't keep my eyes open, then I may have been regretful and wish I'd done things differently. That gave me the courage to take the physics class, which gave me the courage to accept that I was forcing the pre-medical track onto myself and wasn't nearly as enthused about general medicine as I was about mental health. As I said, at the time, I was under the impression that medical school was the way to go for an advanced degree in psychology. To me, a

PhD was for teaching positions only, and had nothing to do with the medical field. Turns out, I can still do rotations in a neurology or psychiatric department.

# 11

# What's the Purpose?

My love for psychology is well established. Sure, the classes are interesting, the topics are complex, and there are several components that can interconnect to create an astounding research experiment. But being able to take a heart out of one person's body, put it into someone else's, and get it to work is pretty darn interesting and complex as well. This leads me to a question that defines my passion: How does this intricate dance between the brain and our actions shape my own sense of purpose?

Answering this was eye-opening for me. Let's explore this concept. Think about a chest cold. That's enough to call out of work, get paid time off, and it may even excuse a bad attitude one day. Now think about if someone just breaks down, starts crying, and feels out of control. Now they are deemed all of these terms that I don't even want to list, because they are far too stigmatizing. Now, think about being a minority who already has plenty of stereotypes to worry about. Combining those two factors together can keep many people from reaching out, cause many people to suffer in silence, and cause a long chain of unfortunate events.

Now, that brings us to what some subconsciously consider "ideal" mental illnesses. Some people have a completely negative view of mental illness. Others see small amounts of anxiety as something that happens. Then, there are people who think that having a mental illness defines you. Lastly, you have people who are uneducated about the matter and choose to compare someone's case to what they "think" an ideal case of [said illness] looks like.

We all go through things, and some more than others. Therefore, we cannot expect everyone to know exactly what the cognitive elements of depression with comorbid anxiety are. But we can destigmatize the subject matter. We can educate one another about why it is important to do regular check-ups, even if you are "fine." I believe it is also important to get away from labels. Sure, someone with anxiety shouldn't be confused with someone with depression, at least not in the treatment modality, due to the varying nature of the two. However, we are not treating the disorder itself, but rather the underlying causes and symptoms. With this mentality, we are able to understand the inner workings of the mind and address the behavioral and biological changes that it may be causing.

I am no doctor, nor have I read any of my MCAT books outside of the one that touches on behavior and psychology. But I did watch my grandmother lose her life right in front of me from her diagnosis of diabetes. Did the doctors tell her she needed to treat her diabetes? No, the treatment focused on her kidney failure, cardiovascular disease, and poor circulation to some of her extremities as symptoms of her diabetes. Let me break it down. At the beginning stages of her diagnosis, she was taking insulin shots, which focused on her blood sugar levels. Her kidney failure led to the need for dialysis. Her cardiovascular disease led to the need of a pacemaker. Her poor circulation led to the amputation of half of one of her legs. This further addresses that specific conditions of a disease or disorder are targeted during treatment and no one gets caught up with the umbrella diagnosis term. My great-grandmother, the mother of my grandmother in the scenario I just described, was also diagnosed with diabetes, yet she is still living, past the age of her daughter with the same disease. Those are two different cases, with two completely different outcomes from the same diagnosis of diabetes.

If we think about mental illness in that way, that changes the game completely. One person with anxiety may benefit from talk therapy for a few months and be good to go. Someone else with anxiety may experience concentration issues and be going down a slippery slope trying to keep up with their anxious thoughts. That does not make any case more worthy of awareness than another.

Having heard some of the snarky remarks and comments about those with mental illness, hearing negative phrases thrown around as jokes, and listening to people confidently tell one another, "You don't have depression, you're just being dramatic," has fueled my drive to understand the variety of overlaps between disorders. My goal is to educate others about these complex topics.

That, that was my purpose. The reason I felt such an overwhelming feeling toward finding the perfect career for me and crafting this perfect plan is because I wanted to do something different. I had never heard of the specialty *neuropsychology.* Yet, here I am hoping to become a clinical neuropsychologist. I ask so many questions regarding the matter, because it is not often talked about. When you ask someone what they want to be, they don't tell you all of the background work they had to do to come to that decision. Technically speaking, I'd be a clinical psychologist with specialized training in clinical neuropsychology later on. From there, I can choose to take the board exam to be referred to as a clinical neuropsychologist. Still, that is my personal insight and details for what *I* want to do. Meaning, my purpose runs deep. Personally, I have the same respect for a licensed psychologist as I do for a neuropsychiatrist. One of which some places allow you to be with a master's, the other which requires you to go to medical school and do specialized training. Still, we all just want to help people.

This is how I realized that my purpose was to delve into the depths of the mind and integrate that understanding with what I learn about the brain. There is no prize for getting specialized training. Some say you get paid more based on your title, but it all comes down to where you work in my opinion. Sure, certain degrees hold more weight in certain fields, but no one really cares how you get where you get... at least I don't. Once I started comparing myself to my old self, I realized that life was golden. I realized that I was happy with who I'd become and did not feel the need to compare myself to others. I was pushing Lauren to be better and to do better.

Though we don't talk about it, we all have days where we just feel overwhelmed and depleted by our inner thoughts. From the outside looking in, life seems perfect. Inside our heads, we see so much more, beyond what can be seen or put into words. I want to be the person on the other end of the table when someone needs help putting those thoughts into words. Better yet, I want to be the person who helps someone understand their inner thoughts without them having to tell me every word or image that comes to mind. There are studies that touch on the biological changes of mental health disorders. Of course, not everyone cares about that and some of us just want to be better. Well, there is nothing wrong with that either. My goal is to use my specialized training to be the best psychologist that I can be and provide the biggest impact for everyone to live the productive life that they aspire to live.

# 12

# The Journey

The point wasn't that I crafted my ideal plan, nor was it that I knew exactly what I wanted to do. Sure, I have my plans, multiple versions of them actually. Yet, there are still many gaps for the journey itself. As I write this, I am not certain who my PhD advisor will be, if I will in fact be applying for admission next fall, or if I will get my master's degree from Georgia Tech. What I do know is that I want to get my PhD, the field I want it to be in, the career that I am targeting, and the things that I am able to do *now* to get closer to achieving these goals. Just a few months ago I was anxiously planning out my life, making 10-20 year plans, including what I would do in my daily schedules. Such a detailed plan, yet it did not advance me much further than it would have if it just included "PhD, fellowship, practice, and academia." Yet, each category took up half a page, being so detailed.

The key word was outline. I needed an outline of my ideal scenario and to think of the little details, rather than viciously write them all down. I needed to let my mind wander and understand the importance of different opportunities I came across. Rather than fast tracking and overwhelming myself, wasting time trying to research every clinical neuropsychologist who practices on neurological and psychological diseases, being fatigued from overplanning, and feeling like I was a complete failure, I was able to enjoy welcoming freshman to college. I was able to dedicate time to being a teaching assistant and ask all the questions I wanted about academia, rather than trying to find answers somewhere online. I was able to allow the process of finding an invaluable research advisor to run its course, rather than rushing to get my PhD. I was able to enjoy the field that I am ultimately dedicating my life to.

My love for the field has actually grown substantially since taking on this new outlook. I was able to truly explore my interests. Sure, I do find my mind wandering about the "what ifs," but I make sure to remind myself *what is.* By doing this, I have reviewed my course loads to allow myself time to give back to the Georgia Tech community. I have provided myself ample amount of time to choose one of the various paths I have planned out. Of course, the planning did come in handy. It was just that I did it far too much. I was making things overcomplicated by going into the depths of what time I will teach a class in twenty years.

The bottom line is, having a plan was nice, until it wasn't. I needed to set boundaries for myself. I needed to tell myself that I did not have to have all of the answers *right now* and that they would come. Sure enough, taking this step back allowed me to ask myself different questions. I was able to re-evaluate how I could accomplish these long-term goals, rather than what I will do in my day-to-day life *after* accomplishing said goals.

By embracing this wonderful journey that I am on, I have opened up so many doors. In the rush, I overlooked being a transition seminar team leader and vaguely considered being a teaching assistant. All I saw was research and clinical experience. I did not truly read the emails that were coming to me about these opportunities, as I knew in my mind where I wanted to be, even after switching from pre-med to pre-grad. I didn't know anything. When I say anything, I mean anything about the field itself. Sure, I could tell you all about the cognitive processes and amygdala changes in certain disorders. If you ask me a question, I might elaborate on the role of the anterior cingulate cortex, just not in front of my mom. Yet, I am still a bit uncertain about the complete process and intricate details after graduate school. Am I worried about it? No, not at all. Why? Because I know that I have a general outline, several career possibilities within this outline, and am still following the path to lead me to my ultimate goal with plenty of room to let things fall into place.

Now, I am soon to start my role as a teaching assistant under a clinical psychologist whom I can ask all of my super technical questions to. I am also leading a transition seminar, which has helped me understand the struggles of students who have no idea what they want to do in ten years, like my little sister. I have been open to asking questions, even if they are far fetched, as some would say. This led me to visit a lab, where I can finally find someone to talk to about anhedonia and fMRI scans of depressed patients. When the summer started, I had no idea that I'd be visiting a lab, learning how to be a teaching assistant, or that I'd be looking for personal development opportunities such as QPR training to prevent suicide. Before, I was goal-driven. Now, I am **purpose-driven**. By letting my purpose drive me, I am able to find interest in waking up early enough to beat traffic and make it to a training, then go to a lab, to still have energy to come home and cook dinner. Sure, there are times when I feel overwhelmed and exhausted. Those are the times that I rely on my boundaries to avoid criticizing myself for something I literally could stop doing at any given moment and be just fine.

Now, I am living. When I say living, I mean living, driven, excited, and so much more. Of course, stress-free will likely never be on my list as someone who loves organization and future planning. However, I can say that I do feel much less stressed. I can continue my planning, while leaving gaps for the journey. I can continue my journey, while allowing myself to explore new opportunities. I can use these new opportunities to fill in the gaps, learn more about myself, and tailor this plan so that it gets closer and closer to my goal. By incrementing, I give my mind time to wander, in a good way. I can allow myself to go to sleep without pulling out my computer and starting this plan all over when I have a new idea. I have now added multiple things to my resume, enjoyed knowing that I will likely be faced with something different the next day, and been eager to see what each day holds, essentially ushering me closer and closer to becoming Dr. Reed.

*My quick guide to success:*

- Plan lightly and explore similar careers.
- Network, reach out, and make advising appointments.
- Explore a variety of classes and job options.
- Explore volunteer opportunities in your field of interest.
- Highlight likes and dislikes.
- Use each opportunity to grow.
- Revisit the conversation about the "ideal" opportunity.
- Learn the steps to get there.
- Leave space to explore extracurricular opportunities.
- Talk to people in the field and talk to more advisors.
- Connect with students who survived this transition.
- Ask questions and be confident.
- Most of all allow time to have some fun.

When the field does not look so fun and seems dreadful, meet with an advisor, ask questions, and reach out. You may simply be using the wrong title to describe your dream job...I know I was. You got this!

# About the Author

Lauren Reed is a passionate scholar, writer, and speaker dedicated to helping others overcome imposter syndrome and limited mindsets to achieve their full potential. Currently studying psychology at the Georgia Institute of Technology, Lauren is on a mission to become a clinical neuropsychologist and continue to help others on a deeper level.

With a keen interest in the human mind and behavior, Lauren has dedicated her studies and research to understanding how we can overcome mental barriers and limiting beliefs to lead happier, more fulfilling lives. Her work has been recognized for its impact and significance, and she has been invited to speak at various conferences and events to share her knowledge and experience.

Beyond her academic pursuits, Lauren is also an avid writer and blogger, where she shares her insights on personal growth and development. Her writing has been featured in various publications and platforms, and her work has inspired many to take action toward their goals and dreams.

Lauren lives in Atlanta with her loving family, including her mom and dad, baby sister London, and beloved dog Bunny. When she's not studying or writing, Lauren enjoys spending time with her family, exploring new places, and trying out new recipes in the kitchen.

With her passion for helping others and her dedication to her craft, Lauren is a rising star in the field of psychology, and her work is sure to make a lasting impact on those she comes into contact with.

www.ingramcontent.com/pod-product-compliance
Lightning Source LLC
Chambersburg PA
CBHW031256120626
46545CB00007B/2849